D0246089

Little Creatures
Ladybirds

by Lisa J. Amstutz

raintree

a Capstone company — publishers for children

Raintree is an imprint of Capstone Global Library Limited, a company incorporated in England and Wales having its registered office at 264 Banbury Road, Oxford, OX2 7DY – Registered company number: 6695582

www.raintree.co.uk
myorders@raintree.co.uk

Editorial Credits
Carrie Braulick Sheely, editor; Juliette Peters, designer; Wanda Winch, media researcher; Tori Abraham, production specialist

ISBN 978-1-4747-2505-7 (hardback)
20 19 18 17 16
10 9 8 7 6 5 4 3 2 1
ISBN 978-1-4747-2509-5 (paperback)
21 20 19 18 17
10 9 8 7 6 5 4 3 2 1

British Library Cataloguing in Publication Data
A full catalogue record for this book is available from the British Library.

Acknowledgements
We would like to thank the following for permission to reproduce photographs:
Ardea.com: Steve Hopkin, 11; Dreamstime: Bereta, 9, Laozhang, 19, Nancykennedy, 15; Shutterstock: Andre Mueller, 17, Bachkova Natalia, 22, Dennis van de Water, 7, Evgeniya Tiplyashina, cover, 5, Henrik Larsson, 13, icarmen13, 1, Igor Sokolov (breeze), back cover, Jan Miko, 21, LianeM, daisy background used throughout book, Maxal Tamor, 20, Oleksandr Kozachenko, 6, picsfive, note design, Valentina Proskurina, back cover (ladybug), 3 (all), 24

Every effort has been made to contact copyright holders of material reproduced in this book. Any omissions will be rectified in subsequent printings if notice is given to the publisher.

All the Internet addresses (URLs) given in this book were valid at the time of going to press. However, due to the dynamic nature of the Internet, some addresses may have changed, or sites may have changed or ceased to exist since publication. While the author and publisher regret any inconvenience this may cause readers, no responsibility for any such changes can be accepted by either the author or the publisher.

Contents

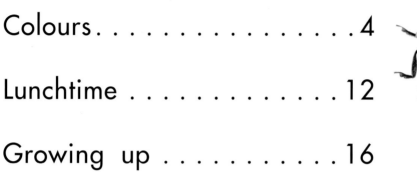

Colours

Look! There is a ladybird!

It is red with black spots.

There are about 5,000 types of ladybird. Some types are yellow and black. Some types are black and orange.

Ladybirds have four wings.

Two wings are hard and shiny.

Two wings are soft and clear.

Ladybirds have six legs.

They make stinky goo.

It keeps hungry animals away.

Lunchtime

Two antennae smell food.

Most ladybirds eat

small insects.

antennae

Ladybirds are helpers!

They eat pests.

Pests hurt plants.

Growing up

A ladybird lays tiny eggs.

She hides them under a leaf.

A bumpy larva comes out of each egg. It grows. It sheds its skin.

The larva attaches to a leaf. It is now a pupa. The pupa turns into an adult. It flies away. Goodbye!

pupa

Glossary

adult fully grown

antenna thin body part on the head of an insect

larva insect at a stage of development between an egg and an adult

pest animal that harms plants or crops humans need by eating them

shed let something fall off

Read more

Ladybirds (Creepy Crawlies), Sian Smith (Raintree, 2013)
Let's Look for Minibeasts: A Natural History Activity Book,
Caz Buckingham and Andrea Pinnington (Fine Feather
Press, 2015)
Minibeast Body Parts (Animal Body Parts), Clare Lewis
(Raintree, 2015)

Websites

www.bbc.co.uk/cbeebies/shows/mini-beast-adventure-
with-jess
Go on a minibeast adventure with Jess, and discover the
minibeasts that are on your doorstep!

www.woodlandtrust.org.uk
naturedetectives/activities/2015/06/minibeast-mansion/
Design and build your own minibeast mansion!

Comprehension questions

1. What do ladybirds eat?
2. How do ladybirds help plants?

Index